DARTH VADER™

ISBN: 978-1-4521-0850-6

Manufactured by Starlite Development, Wu Jiang Qu,
Shaoguan, China, in October 2015.
Designed by Michael Morris

10 9 8 7 6 5

Chronicle Books LLC
680 Second Street
San Francisco, California 94107
www.chroniclebooks.com

www.starwars.com

DARTH VADER

TOGETHER WE CAN RULE THE GALAXY

CHRONICLE BOOKS

San Francisco

THE MAN WHO WOULD ONE DAY TERRORIZE THE GALAXY

as Darth Vader was born Anakin Skywalker, a slave boy who lived with his mother on the remote desert world of Tatooine. Young Anakin was mechanically gifted and demonstrated a natural ability to anticipate events before they happened—an instinct Jedi Master Qui-Gon Jinn quickly recognized as the trait of a Jedi. Qui-Gon became so convinced of Anakin's abilities with the Force that he declared his belief to the Jedi Council that Anakin was the Chosen One of Jedi prophecy—he who would restore balance to the Force.

But Master Yoda felt conflict in the boy—conflict that might one day consume the young Jedi and seduce him to the dark side of the Force. "Fear is the path to the dark side," Yoda had warned. "Fear leads to anger . . . anger leads to hate . . . hate leads to suffering." Anakin's fear of losing his mother—or anyone close to him—might cause him to embrace impulses rising from his darker emotions, such as anger, aggression, and hate, aspects of the dark side of the Force. Despite Yoda's warnings, the Jedi Council cautiously allowed Anakin to be trained as a Jedi, determined to keep a close watch on the boy's progress.

Under the instruction of Master Obi-Wan Kenobi, Anakin began to find the ways of the Jedi increasingly at odds with what he regarded as strengths—he was impulsive on the battlefield and fiercely protective of those closest to him. "The fear of loss is a path to the dark side," Yoda cautioned.

This internal conflict grew more pronounced when Anakin failed to save his mother from savage Tusken Raiders on Tatooine, deeply regretting the day he left her to become a Jedi Knight. His growing fear of loss, and its effect on his forbidden love for Padmé Amidala, was making him increasingly vulnerable to the dark side of the Force.

Chancellor Palpatine, who instructed the young Jedi under the auspices of friendship, had secretly plotted Anakin's path to the dark side, setting in motion events that would nudge the unsuspecting Jedi ever closer to his destiny as a Sith. Once Palpatine revealed himself as an agent of the dark side—a Sith Lord—he was able to seduce Anakin with hints of wisdom that could prevent those closest to him from dying. Vowing his allegiance to Palpatine, Anakin Skywalker became the Sith Lord Darth Vader.

Among the first casualties of Anakin's turn to the dark side was Padmé, the secret wife he had sought to protect with his newfound Sith powers. Her loss fully consumed the Dark Lord, now clad in the black robes and armor of Darth Vader, with rage and aggression. But not all was lost—a shred of the very feelings he had been forbidden to keep as a Jedi remained deep within, hidden from the penetrating glare of Vader's new master, Emperor Palpatine.

When Palpatine discovered Anakin had secretly fathered a Force-sensitive son—Luke Skywalker—he ordered Vader to hunt the boy down and destroy him. But Vader offered an alternative—if the young Skywalker could be turned to the dark side, he would become a powerful ally. Seeing the possibility of a more powerful apprentice to replace Vader, Palpatine agreed.

Doggedly pursuing Luke across the galaxy, Vader finally captured his son and brought him before the Emperor. Unlike Vader, Luke was able to restrain himself from the seduction of the dark side. Enraged, Palpatine unleashed a destructive attack of Force lightning, overwhelming the young Jedi. As Vader watched his son writhe in pain, long-buried feelings of regret and compassion stirred within the Dark Lord, compelling him to turn on his master and hurl him into the depths of a reactor shaft. Palpatine was dead, and with him, his grip on Vader's destiny.

Vader—Anakin once again—had found a path, a balance, between the teachings of the Jedi and the seductions of the Sith, fulfilling his destiny as the one who would restore balance to the Force.

The Force is with you, young Skywalker.
But you are not a Jedi yet.

I am your father.

I find your lack of
faith disturbing.

ANAKIN
And when I got to them, we went into . . .
aggressive negotiations.

PADMÉ
"Aggressive negotiations,"
what's that?

ANAKIN
Negotiations with a lightsaber.

VADER
He is here . . .

TARKIN
Obi-Wan Kenobi! What makes
you think so?

VADER
A tremor in the Force. The last time I felt it
was in the presence of my old Master.

TARKIN
Surely he must be dead by now.

VADER
Don't underestimate the Force.

This will be a day long remembered. It has seen the end of Kenobi. It will soon see the end of the Rebellion.

VADER

The circle is now complete.
When I left you, I was but the learner;
now I am Master.

BEN

Only a master of evil, Darth.

The Emperor will show you the true nature
of the Force. He is your Master now.

ANAKIN

I'm becoming more powerful than any Jedi has ever dreamed of.

EMPEROR

We have a new enemy—Luke Skywalker.

VADER

Yes, my Master.

EMPEROR

He could destroy us. . . . The Force is
strong with him. The son of Skywalker
must not become a Jedi.

VADER

If he could be turned, he would become
a powerful ally.

EMPEROR

Yes. Yes. He would be a great asset.
Can it be done?

VADER

He will join us or die, Master.

The Force is strong with this one!

Don't be too proud of this technological terror you've constructed. The ability to destroy a planet is insignificant next to the power of the Force.

Obi-Wan has taught you well. You have
controlled your fear . . . now release your anger.

LUKE

Your thoughts betray you, Father. I feel
the good in you . . . the conflict.

VADER

There is no conflict . . . If you will not
fight, then you will meet your destiny.

You may dispense with the pleasantries, Commander. I'm here to put you back on schedule.

I am altering the deal. Pray I don't alter it any further.

EMPEROR
There is a great disturbance in the Force.

VADER

I have felt it.

Join me, and together we can rule the galaxy as father and son.

There'll be no one to stop us this time.

If you only knew the power
of the dark side.

VADER

Impressive . . . most impressive.